SOLVE IT WITH SCIENCE!

SOLIDS, LIQUIDS, AND GASES

BY ELIZA NODES

KidHaven PUBLISHING

Published in 2026 by
KidHaven Publishing, an Imprint of Greenhaven Publishing, LLC
2544 Clinton St., Buffalo, NY 14224

Written by: Eliza Nodes
Edited by: Noah Leatherland
Designed by: Rob Delph

Cataloging-in-Publication Data

Names: Nodes, Eliza.
Title: Solids, liquids, and gases / Eliza Nodes.
Description: Buffalo, NY : KidHaven Publishing, 2026. | Series: Solve it with science! | Includes glossary and index.
Identifiers: ISBN 9781534551916 (pbk.) | ISBN 9781534551923 (library bound) | ISBN 9781534551930 (ebook)
Subjects: LCSH: Matter--Properties--Juvenile literature. | Solids--Juvenile literature. | Gases--Juvenile literature. | Liquids--Juvenile literature.
Classification: LCC QC173.36 N634 2026 | DDC 530.4--dc23

Printed in China

CPSIA compliance information: Batch #QW26KH: For further information contact Greenhaven Publishing LLC at 1-844-317-7404.

Photo Credits – Images courtesy of Shutterstock.com, unless otherwise stated.

Cover & Recurring – Avalepsap, Subbotina Anna, Proonty, MartiBstock, AAVAA, ZipDesign, Olga PaHa, keenani. 2–3 – ad_serpent, puha dorin, irin-k, n_defender, Photoongraphy, trancedrumer. 4–5 – Igor Normann, Negro Elkha, ElenaChelysheva, Nualanong, Dream01. 6–7 – Igor Normann, Negro Elkha, ElenaChelysheva, Nualanong, Dream01. 8–9 – Anton Serkin, BongrakArt, ifong, ILYA AKINSHIN, Dream01. 10–11 – K-FK, Volodymyr TVERDOKHLIB, Artem Oleshko, Dream01. 12–13 – V_Lisovoy, v74. 14–15 – New Africa, Vltava. 16–17 – Harmony Video Production, Machmarsky. 18–19 – Harmony Video Production, Machmarsky. 20–21 – Sansanorth, New Africa. 22–23 – Brian Mueller, Elnur, Maria_Petrishina.

CONTENTS

PAGE 4 Particles Everywhere
PAGE 6 What Is a Solid?
PAGE 8 What Is a Liquid?
PAGE 10 What Is a Gas?
PAGE 12 Changing States
PAGE 14 Solid to Liquid
PAGE 16 Liquid to Gas
PAGE 18 Gas to Liquid
PAGE 20 Dissolving
PAGE 22 Activities
PAGE 24 Glossary and Index

Words that look like this can be found in the glossary on page 24.

PARTICLES EVERYWHERE

Everything is made of tiny things called particles. Particles are tiny pieces of matter. Matter is everything that can be seen and touched. Particles make up tables, chairs, books, toys, everything!

Solids, liquids, and gases are three different states of matter. Particles of matter behave differently when they make up a solid, a liquid, or a gas.

WHAT IS A SOLID?

Solids are things that have a fixed shape. That means that they do not change shape. Materials such as wood, metal, and glass are solids. Sugar, sand, and salt are very small solids.

The particles that make up solids are tightly packed together. This is what gives solids their fixed shape. Solids can be cut or broken into pieces.

WHAT IS A LIQUID?

Liquids do not have a fixed shape. Liquids take the shape of whatever container they are poured into. Water, honey, and oil are all examples of liquids.

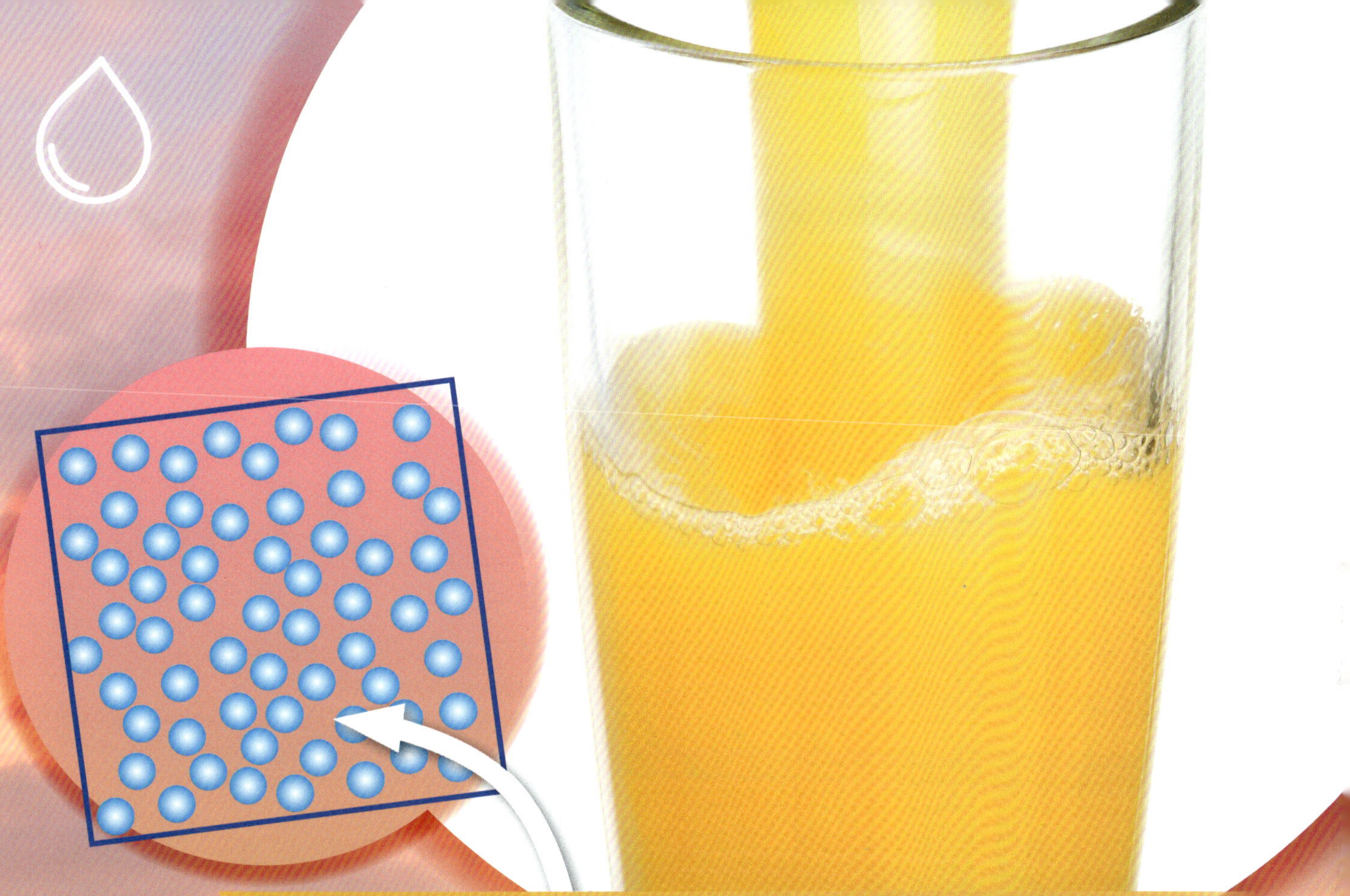

PARTICLES ARE CLOSE BUT MOVE AROUND

The particles that make up a liquid are close together. However, they still have space to move around each other. This is why liquids change shape.

WHAT IS A GAS?

Gases do not have a fixed shape. Gases spread out and fill the space around them. Examples of gases include steam and oxygen. Air is made up of many different gases.

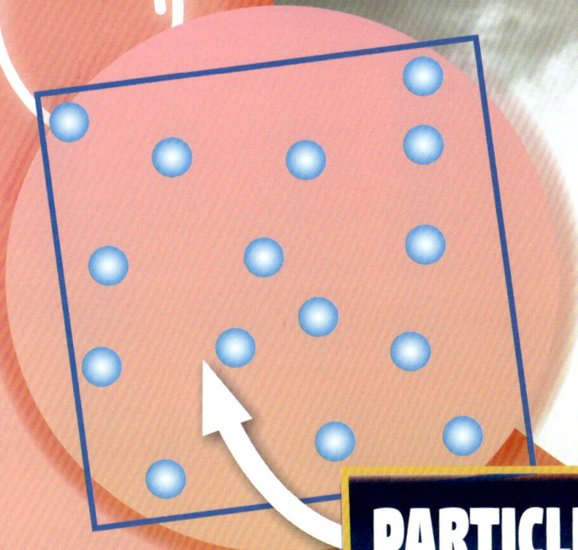

PARTICLES ARE FREE TO MOVE AROUND

Gases are made up of particles that are spread out. Particles in gases move around in all directions. This means that gases can fill large spaces and squeeze through small gaps.

CHANGING STATES

Most things can exist as a solid, liquid, and a gas. Their state of matter can change. Changing something's state of matter usually uses energy, such as heat or pressure.

METAL BEING HEATED INTO A LIQUID

Energy changes how particles behave. Particles with less energy move around less. Particles with lots of energy move around more and spread out.

SOLID TO LIQUID

When a solid is heated, its particles gain energy. This makes them move and break away from each other. This causes the solid to melt into a liquid. Different solids melt at different temperatures.

BUTTER MELTING

Ice is frozen water. When ice starts to warm up, it melts into liquid water. When water starts to cool again, it turns back into solid ice. This is called freezing.

LIQUID TO GAS

When particles in a liquid are warmed up, they move faster and in different directions. The particles spread out so much that the liquid turns into a gas. This is called evaporation.

When water gets warmed up, its particles gain more energy. They move around more and spread out farther. This turns the water into a gas called water vapor.

GAS TO LIQUID

Condensation is when a gas turns into a liquid. This happens when a gas cools down. Colder temperatures make the gas particles slow down and move around less.

CONDENSATION IN A KETTLE

Water vapor condenses when it touches a cold surface. The cold surface cools down the particles in the gas. This removes energy from the particles and turns the water vapor into liquid water.

DISSOLVING

Dissolving is when a solid breaks down inside a liquid. The solid particles break apart. They move in between the liquid particles. This means the solid has dissolved.

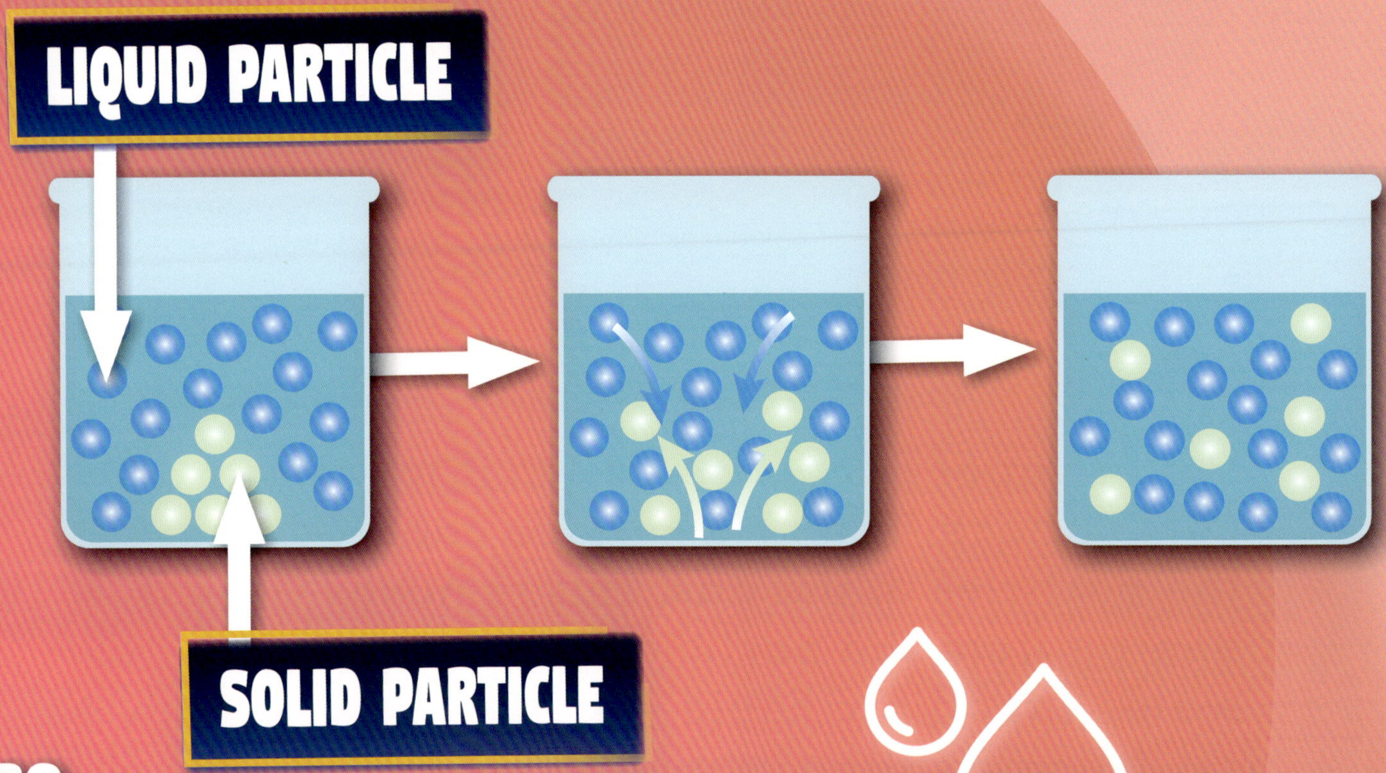

DID YOU KNOW?

Even if it is dissolved, a solid object is still solid.

Solids dissolve faster if the particles have more energy. Sugar dissolves faster in hot water because the heat gives the particles more energy. Stirring the water also gives the particles more energy.

ACTIVITIES

Here are some activities to explore solids, liquids, and gases.

THINK ABOUT IT

Fill in the empty spaces below with the correct word.

LESS | MELTS | GAS

Ice _____ to become water.

Oxygen is a type of _______.

When particles cool down, they have _____ energy.

Answers: 1. melts, 2. gas, 3. less

DO AN EXPERIMENT

Put an ice cube in three separate bowls. Put each bowl in a different place. After a few minutes, take a look. Have the ice cubes started to melt? Which one has melted the most?

GLOSSARY

ENERGY a type of power, such as light or heat, that can be used to do something

MATERIALS things from which objects are made

OXYGEN a natural gas that living things need in order to survive

SURFACE the outside layer of something

TEMPERATURES measurements of how hot or cold something is

WATER VAPOR water that is in the form of a gas

INDEX

ENERGY 12–14, 17, 19, 21–22
ICE 15, 22–23
MATTER 4–5, 12
METALS 6, 12
OXYGEN 10, 22
SUGAR 6, 21
WATER 8, 15, 17, 19, 21–22
WOOD 6